36 - 50 ✓

PHIL STERN'S HOLLYWOOD

PHIL STERN's
HOLLYWOOD

PHOTOGRAPHS ———

1940–1979

Phil Stern

ALFRED A. KNOPF   NEW YORK

1993

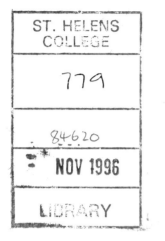
THIS IS A BORZOI BOOK
PUBLISHED BY ALFRED A. KNOPF, INC.

Library of Congress Cataloging-in-Publication Data
Stern, Phil.
Phil Stern's Hollywood : photographs, 1940–1979 / Phil Stern. —
1st ed.
p.   cm.
ISBN 0-394-58110-5
1. Motion picture actors and actresses—California—Hollywood
(Los Angeles)—Portraits. I. Title. II. Title: Hollywood.
PN2285.S7194 1993
791.43´6520396073—dc20   92-46282
                                                    CIP

Manufactured in the United States of America
Published November 3, 1993
Second printing before publication

To the memory of my oldest son, pilot Philip Carl "Flip" Stern,
who was killed in an air crash at age twenty-three.
And to his very-much-alive sister Lata and brothers Peter and Tom,
their wives Lisa and Bonnie, and my grandchildren, Sean, Dustin,
Ashley, Courtney, Tommy, Katie, and Samantha.
Such a roster of progeny requires more talent than mine alone:
well-deserved thanks must go to the lovely Rosemae Lindou.

ACKNOWLEDGMENTS

This book's four-year gestation period required the active hands-on assistance of a very special group of photo gurus. Vital was the deft selective hand of Vicky Wilson, who shielded me from most of umpteen self-inflicted wounds. Also helpful were David Fahey and Vicki Gold Levi.

For further help and encouragement, I must thank Susan Bluttman, Lata Ryan, Lesa Sawahata, and Mary Garrett; also, Charlie Holland (*Premiere*), Dan Okrent (*Life*), Doris Brautigan (*Entertainment Weekly*), Carin Wong (*Entertainment Tonight*), Blanche Williamson (*People*), Jennifer Crandall (*US*), Françoise Joyes (*Paris Match*), Jim Moret (*CNN's Show Business*), Grazia Neri (*Grazia*), Dave Jampel (*Imperial Press*), David Bealing (*P.I.P. Ltd. London*), Nadia Danilova (*Mosfilm Moscow*), Nicky Akehurst (Akehurst Gallery, London), Terry McDonell (*Esquire*), and Wayne Lawson (*Vanity Fair*).

I would also like to thank Ashley Ward III, for finding the photographs of John Wayne that appear on pages 9 and 11; Heywood Broun, who taught me not to cross a picket line; publisher Daniel S. Gillmor, who found me working in a Canal Street photoengraving shop and hired me for his magazine *Friday*; artist and art director Sam Shaw, who taught me about graphic arts; Harry Henderson of *Collier's*, who demonstrated that a thousand words could damn well prevail over a photograph; and David Golding, former editor of *Stars and Stripes* and Hollywood publicist.

PHIL STERN'S HOLLYWOOD

Bobby Darin, *Pressure Point,* 1962

Marilyn Monroe, from Samuel Goldwyn's window, 1958, during the filming of *Some Like It Hot*

Slim Pickens during the filming of Steven Spielberg's *1941*, 1979

John Ford during the filming of *The Alamo*, 1960

John Wayne and John Ford, *The Alamo*, 1960

John Wayne, Acapulco, mid-1950s. There have been a number of superb photographs that, due to ineptitude, being asleep at the shutter, or simple fear, I have failed to capture. During the filming of *True Grit*, John Wayne had a very special closeup horse called Twinkle Toes. They'd been a pair for years; whenever Wayne was head-and-head with a horse, and wherever galloping closeups of the star were required, that was the horse he used. Twinkle Toes aged, just like Wayne. At one point, getting ready for the epic closeup shots in *True Grit*, a makeup man was doing his number on Wayne—softening up the lines in his face, darkening the white and gray hair. Fifteen feet behind them another makeup man was doing the same thing to Twinkle Toes. (He was well beyond the age at which the ASPCA allowed horses to work.) I struggled with the temptation to capture that shot but didn't dare.

John Wayne, *The Alamo*, 1960

Hedda Hopper and Margot Fonteyn at a party given by John Wayne, mid-1950s

Hopper with Frank Capra and William Wellman

Rock Hudson and Susan Talbot at the Universal Studios Acting School, 1953. Hudson had recently quit his job as a truck driver to sign a $100-a-week contract with Universal. He took the prerequisite studio acting classes; Tony Curtis and Jayne Mansfield were among his classmates.

Jean Negulesco, his wife Dusty, Sam Goldwyn, and "Prince" Mike Romanoff
at Samuel Goldwyn's, Beverly Hills, mid-1950s

Gary Cooper with his wife Rocky and their daughter Maria, poolside,
Beverly Hills, mid-1950s

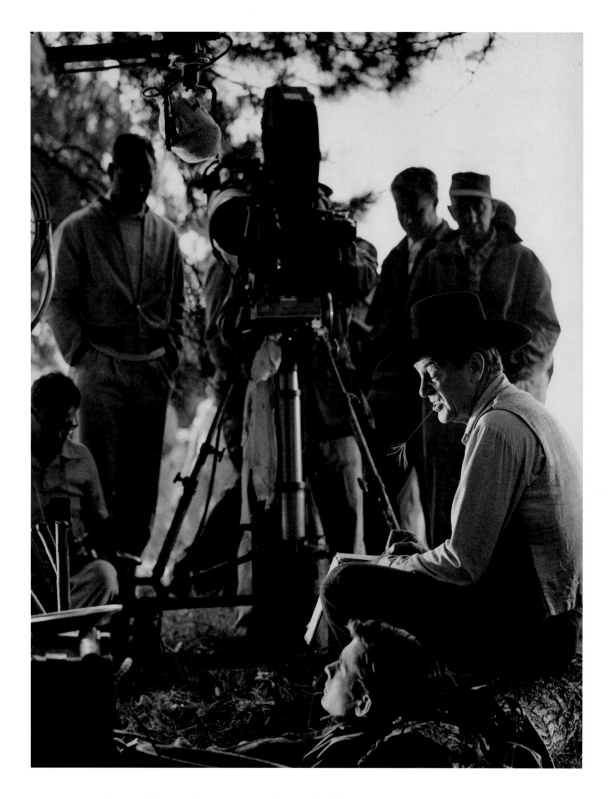

Tony Perkins and Gary Cooper during the filming of *Friendly Persuasion,* 1956

William Wyler, *Friendly Persuasion*, 1956

William Wyler, Charlton Heston, Carroll Baker, Jean Simmons, and
Gregory Peck during the making of *The Big Country,* 1958

Vladimir Posner (far left), Susan Strasberg, her brother John, George Stevens, Jr., Susan Oliver,
Stanley Kramer, and Sidney Poitier at the Moscow Film Festival, Lenin Stadium, 1967

Kirk Douglas, *The War Wagon*, 1967

Natalie Wood at a publicity shoot, 1961. Natalie was close to Maya Plisetskaya, the *prima ballerina assoluta* of the Bolshoi Ballet, and whenever the Bolshoi came to Los Angeles, she would entertain the company.

23

Danny Kaye during the filming of *Hans Christian Andersen*, 1952

Legend of the Lost (1957), Sophia Loren's first big Hollywood film. The movie was shot in the Libyan desert, about five hundred miles south of Tripoli; John Wayne and Rossano Brazzi were the stars. Carlo Ponti was connected with the film. He and Loren weren't yet married, but he sent along a sort of chaperone—a Communist professor of history from Rome University.

Everyone was crazy about Sophia, including the cameraman, Jack Cardiff. Cardiff was so busy lighting Loren, a second camera-man had to be brought in from Rome to see that Wayne and Brazzi were properly lit. The film company shot every day except Sunday, which was my day to get the occasional still shot of Sophia. Cardiff, who was also a still photographer, would pack a camera, tripod, and picnic lunch and disappear with Sophia to photograph her. Where was the chaperone? While all this was going on, Cardiff's wife Julie was on the set. At communal dinners, Cardiff would sit opposite Loren, his wife would sit next to him, and Cardiff would stare at Sophia, ignore his wife, and not eat anything. It was like an Italian comic opera.

Sammy Davis, Jr., mid-1950s. I had an assignment to photograph Davis to show his multiple talents. We didn't have a rehearsal studio with a blank wall to make the shots readable. So we found a building on Hollywood Boulevard that had a low roof edge—we could use the sky as our background. The pictures used in this sequence are three out of maybe three hundred. My technical knowledge of dance was zero; I had to go by instinct. Davis was great. Finally we had the shots, and as we were packing up, he looked at me as if he wanted to do some more. "What's the matter?" I said. "Are you crazy?"

"No," he said. "I love to dance!"

Maria Montez and Jean-Pierre Aumont, *Siren of Atlantis,* 1948. *Collier's* wanted a Hollywood glamour shot of the pair. I struggled with this. I looked at the master of this type of photography, George Hurrell. This is what I came up with.

Alfred Hitchcock in his wine cellar, mid-1960s

Blake Edwards and Robert Wagner during the shooting of *The Pink Panther*, 1963

Audrey Hepburn and John Huston, *The Unforgiven*, 1960. One of the featured players on *The Unforgiven* was an Arabian stallion. After he threw Audrey Hepburn, the film's production was halted for six weeks. When filming resumed, a stunt double for Audrey was doing a leap across a small creek. One of the most dramatic pictures of a leaping horse is taken from a low angle. I lay down at the edge of the creek in the lowest position I could find. I knew where the horse was going to leap and pointed the camera upwards. The horse *did* leap—but something spooked him, and he jumped directly over my body. By some kind of instinct, one hoof landed between my arm and my torso, and another between my legs.

Audie Murphy and John Huston, *The Unforgiven*, 1960. One day I rode out to the location of *The Unforgiven*—Durango, Mexico—with Audie Murphy, Albert Salmi, and Lillian Gish. Suddenly, Murphy told the driver to stop the car. Murphy leapt out of the car, pulled a handgun out of his pocket, and ran over to a gully. We heard shots. He killed an animal that was running—it looked like a dog. When he got back into the car, he said, "Sorry, folks. Okay, let's go." We resumed our drive to the location.

At that point, Lillian Gish said, "Audie, I sometimes think that you're not only juvenile, but *sick*. What did you have to go and shoot that animal for? You're looking for blood! You want to show what a great, tough man you are!" And Murphy said, "Lillian, you remarked upon those lovely little Mexican children that were playing near our hotel. Do you remember how cute those little children were?" She said, "Yes . . . what's that got to do with it?" Murphy replied, "In this part of the country, there are coyotes. From time to time they'll come out of the mountains and find lone children and literally tear them to shreds. Now, would you care to reconsider your feelings about the matter, Miss Gish?" The rest of the trip was rather quiet.

Audie Murphy, *To Hell and Back*, 1955

Veronica Lake during the shooting of *Ramrod*, Grafton, Utah, 1947

Adolph Zukor and Mary Pickford at Zukor's eightieth birthday party, Paramount Studios, 1952

The Warner brothers, mid-1940s

Groucho Marx, Writers' Guild luncheon, 1949

Cantinflas, Jack Lemmon, on the Goldwyn Studios lot, 1959

Brock Peters and Tony Curtis on the Goldwyn Studios lot during the filming
of *Porgy and Bess* and *Some Like It Hot*, 1959

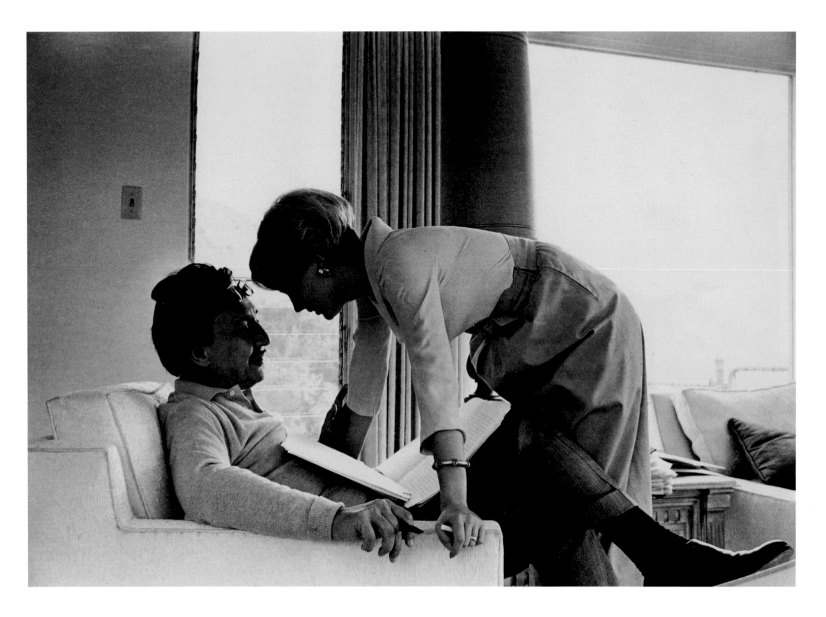

Romain Gary, Jean Seberg, during the filming of *Moment to Moment*, 1966

Yehudi Menuhin and Jack Benny at a Hollywood Bowl benefit, mid-1950s

Jack Benny with Eddie Cantor and George Burns. Benny had a notorious weakness for George Burns' comedy—it was so pronounced that if Burns said "Good morning, Jack," Benny would break into guffaws. If Burns sneezed, Benny would laugh. Anything Burns did was funny to Benny. The reverse was not the case.

Orson Welles, Dolores Costello, and Joseph Cotten on the set of *The Magnificent Ambersons*, 1942

Kim Novak and James Garner during the filming of *Boys' Night Out*, 1962

Mitzi Gaynor (center) on the set of *The Joker Is Wild*, 1957

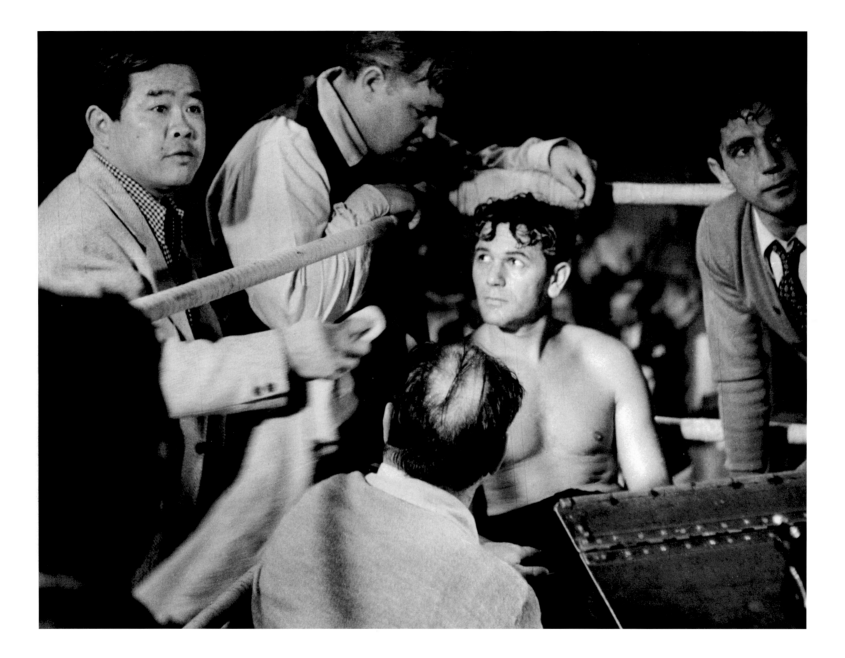

James Wong Howe (left) with John Garfield during the shooting of *Body and Soul*, 1947

Michael Kidd (wearing sneakers) and Joseph Mankiewicz (with pipe), on the set of *Guys and Dolls*, 1955. Kidd was a great choreographer (*Seven Brides for Seven Brothers*, 1954; *Guys and Dolls*, 1955; *Merry Andrew*, 1958). Here, he was in his early forties and had more energy than most of his young dancers. Perhaps it had to do with his lunchtime regimen: First he would do a series of pushups. Then he would eat; each day his lunch consisted of two ripe bananas and a carton of cottage cheese. Finally he would take a short nap on the floor of his dressing room.

Judy Garland during the filming of *A Star Is Born*, 1954

And Garland with Irene Sharaff, who designed the costumes for *A Star Is Born*

Garland with Liza Minelli, Lorna Luft, Joey Luft, mid-1950s

Gordon MacRae, Garland, Lauren Bacall, at Beverly and La Cienega boulevards,
later the site for the Beverly Center, mid-1950s

Bette Davis with her children, mid-1950s

With her daughter Barbara ("B.D."), mid-1950s

John Wayne, Stephen Bogart with his father Humphrey and his mother Lauren Bacall,
Stockton, California, the location for *Blood Alley*, 1955

Lauren Bacall with her daughter Leslie, mid-1950s

Marilyn Monroe with Jack Benny at the Shrine Auditorium, Los Angeles, 1953

Hedda Hopper, 1953

A reading rehearsal of *Whatever Happened to Baby Jane?,* 1962. The director, Bob Aldrich (lower left corner), had a ten-day line-reading rehearsal on the sound stage before shooting. One day I was given twenty minutes to shoot from the catwalk above. At the time, Joan Crawford (top center, with sunglasses) was married to the president of Pepsi-Cola. A Pepsi bottle was next to her at all times, and she occasionally sipped from it. Without ever looking upward, she sensed my movements on the catwalk—and while reading her lines, she would deftly move the bottle and its logo so that none of the other actors would obscure it from my shots.

In this shot, Crawford and Davis (right, with cigarette) seem quite affable. Each had a portable dressing room. Crawford wanted certain adjustments made. She wanted a ledge for her social secretary to put her papers on, and an air-conditioner. She also wanted several other things. She had the men take care of it. As they left Crawford's dressing room with their tools, Davis stood just a few feet away watching. One of the grips said, "Hey, Bette, anything we can do for you?" She said, "No, thank you. Dressing rooms don't *make* pictures." After the wrap each evening, Crawford would leave the sound stage followed by her entourage: hairdresser, makeup man, costumer, social secretary . . . Davis left with just Davis.

Robert Aldrich on the set of *Flight of the Phoenix*, 1965

Mickey Rooney with his son, Beverly Hills, mid-1950s

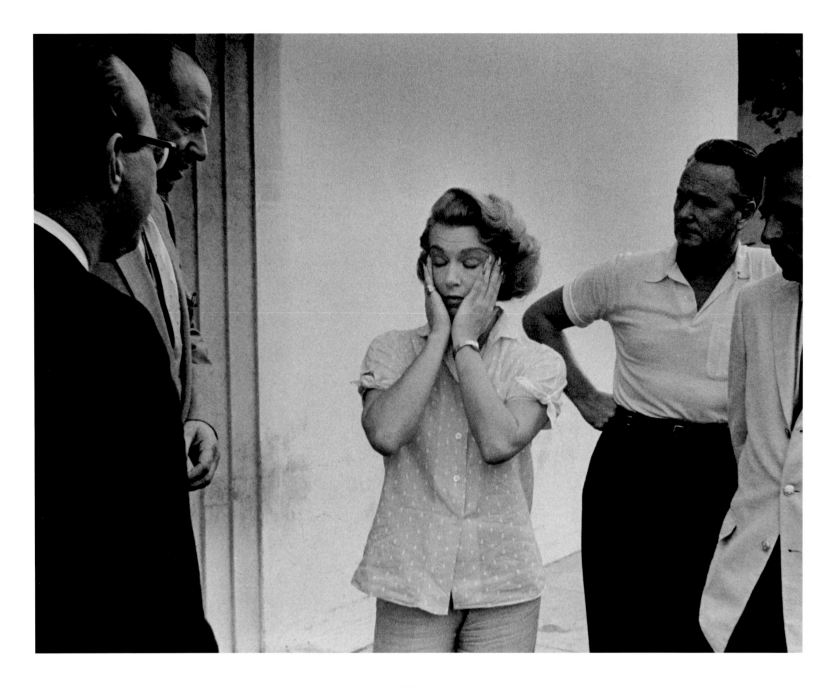

Lana Turner, 1955

Jimmy Durante, 1954. "Goodnight, Mrs. Calabash, wherever you are" was Durante's sign-off on his TV shows. Once, when I was working with him on *The Colgate Comedy Hour*, I asked him who Mrs. Calabash was. This was the story he told me: When he was a struggling young comedian, trying to get work, he lived in Hoboken, New Jersey; Mrs. Calabash was his landlady. At the time, Durante would get an occasional job, or he'd work at a party doing a comedy routine, never making more than a few bucks a night. Often he couldn't pay his rent . . . and Mrs. Calabash would carry him until he got enough money to pay her.

Charlton Heston, Will Rogers estate, Pacific Palisades, mid-1950s

Otto Preminger during the making of *Porgy and Bess*, 1959

Anita Ekberg, 1955

William Holden with Hall Bartlett, a producer, 1958

Lucille Ball, 1948

Esther Williams with June Haver (above) and (opposite) at the Beverly Hills Hotel, 1949

Rita Hayworth and Burt Lancaster during the filming of *Separate Tables*, 1958

Laurence Harvey photographing John Wayne during the making of *The Alamo*, 1960

Dorothy Dandridge (*Porgy and Bess*, 1959) was a staggeringly beautiful actress. She was born and raised in Los Angeles, in an upper-middle-class family. In the late 1940s or early 1950s, one of her uncles died and the family went to Augusta, Georgia, for the funeral. She described the utter terror she felt in that small Southern city—the looks people gave her, the comments they made, the blatant racism and hatred she encountered there.

William Wellman directing *Blood Alley*, Marin County, California, 1955

Rita Moreno, *West Side Story* rehearsal, 1961

Charles Laughton and Billy Wilder during the filming of *Witness for the Prosecution*, 1957

Jane Russell, mid-1950s

Spencer Tracy and Stanley Kramer while filming *Judgment at Nuremberg*, 1961

Ella Fitzgerald, 1961, JFK inaugural ball rehearsal. I was always a little uncomfortable working with Ella Fitzgerald. She was so withdrawn—insecure, I think—though why someone with such incredible God-given talent should be insecure, I have no idea. I worked with her not only at JFK's inaugural ball but in Las Vegas. I was always amazed that her version of relaxation was simply to go down to the nickel slot machines and drop coin after coin into those "one-armed bandits."

Frank Sinatra in his dressing room during the filming of *Guys and Dolls*, 1955

Carolyn Jones, Frank Sinatra, and Frank Capra at a birthday party for
Edward G. Robinson (top right), mid-1950s

Sinatra and John F. Kennedy, inaugural ball, 1961. Sinatra was a great supporter of John F. Kennedy's and was in charge of the entertainment for JFK's inaugural ball, to such a degree that he even performed as an electrician and sound technician. He pulled the wiring, adjusted the microphones, did all the hands-on work required.

Sinatra during the location shooting of *The Devil at 4 O'Clock*, Maui, 1961. In the movie, there was a big sequence of an earthquake and lava flow. This scene didn't require either Sinatra or Spencer Tracy, the film's stars, but it did require a lot of special effects and equipment and extras. And Associated Press in Honolulu sent a cub reporter—he couldn't have been more than twenty or twenty-one—to cover the shooting of this dramatic scene. He was given strict instructions to stay away from Sinatra.

The young reporter asked me to take some photographs for him, and he interviewed the special effects man and the director, Mervyn LeRoy. Sinatra was hovering. Little by little Sinatra got closer, and eventually walked up to the reporter. He asked, "Who are you with?" and very nervously the kid replied, "Associated Press, sir, Honolulu." Sinatra asked the kid if he could buy him lunch.

He told this kid about what he was doing after the film wrapped; he told him what he thought of the film and Mervyn LeRoy; he told the kid about plans he had for the future, concerts he was going to give, other films he was going to make. And he discussed Ava Gardner—which was unheard of!

What I discovered is that Sinatra decides on his own press campaigns—when and where and how he'll release certain information. Of course, the story was wired all over the world.

Sinatra (rear) with Mahalia Jackson, Leonard Bernstein, and Nelson Riddle, 1961

Spencer Tracy during the filming of *The Devil at 4 O'Clock*, 1961. Tracy was dour and introspective and bitter, but the moment the director gave the cue, Tracy erupted and was filled with terror. He was playing a priest whose life and land were threatened.

This photograph of Marlene Dietrich with Tracy in Berlin during the filming of *Judgment at Nuremberg,* 1961, reminds me of when I was assigned to make a panoramic photograph of the entire cast of *Witness for the Prosecution* in the Old Bailey court in London. It required a special type of camera, which I had to rent. And I had to get permission from the studio to take the shot, because the entire cast had to pose for me, and whatever time is taken from the filming of a huge production like *Witness* costs the studio money. The shot was set up, and then,

unexpectedly, something in the camera jammed. I tried desperately to fix it; the assistant director came over and said, "Phil, we've gotta shoot this *now*—we can't wait around." The producer, Arthur Hornblow, Jr., was fit to be tied.

Then I heard a woman's voice with a German accent. It was Marlene Dietrich. "Quiet!" she said. She laid a hand on my shoulder. "Don't let these crass people disturb you. You are an artist. Do what you have to do. Take your time—we'll wait for you."

Mervyn LeRoy (with pipe), Tracy, and Katharine Hepburn, during the filming of
The Devil at 4 O'Clock, Maui, 1961

Marlon Brando, 1955. *Life* wanted me to photograph Brando during the day of the 1954 Academy Awards ceremony (that year he won the Best Actor award for *On the Waterfront*).

We went to the Academy Awards together. Once we had passed through security, Brando said, "Wait a minute. I've got to take a pee," and he left. Time went by; he had disappeared. Finally, I saw a ruckus. There was Brando. The guards would not let him through the security line. I went over and told security who he was, and they let him through.

"What happened?" I said to Brando.

"When I got back, the guard didn't recognize me. And I couldn't figure out how to say, 'I'm Brando. I'm Marlon Brando.'"

Brando during the making of *The Wild One*, 1954, and (opposite) while
filming *The Missouri Breaks*, 1976

James Dean, March 1955. At 7:30 a.m., I was cruising west on Sunset Boulevard, heading for *Life* magazine's photo lab on the Strip. Coming down Laurel Canyon was a crazy motorcyclist who was driving through a red light. We were on a collision course. We both braked and careered through the intersection. I came close to killing him—just a few inches saved his life. I stuck my head out the window, screaming profanities, as he got up off the bike with a dopey grin on his face. It was James Dean.

We ended up having a two-hour breakfast at Schwab's Drug Store, and I invited him over to the *Guys and Dolls* set, where I had a still gallery rigged to shoot Brando and Sinatra. Dean was fascinated by cameras, and came along.

James Dean, Goldwyn Studios, 1955

A NOTE ON THE TYPE

The text of this book was set in Garamond, a modern rendering of the type first cut by Claude Garamond (c. 1480–1561). Garamond was a pupil of Geoffroy Tory and is believed to have based his letters on the Venetian models, although he introduced a number of important differences, and it is to him that we owe the letter we know as "old style." He gave to his letters a certain elegance and a feeling of movement that won for their creator an immediate reputation and the patronage of Francis I of France.

Duotone separations by The Sarabande Press,
New York, New York

Printed by Hull Printing,
Meriden, Connecticut

Bound by Horowitz/Rae,
Fairfield, New Jersey

Designed and composed by
Cassandra J. Pappas